This Is for Me

Illustrated by Fraser Williamson

"This is for me,"
said the fish.

3

"This is for me," said the frog.

"This is for me,"
said the duck.

"This is for me,"
said the boy.

"This is for me,"
said the bird.

"This is for me,"
said the crocodile.